What People Are Saying about Appreciative Inquiry

Appreciative Inquiry is currently revolutionizing the field of organization development.

—Robert Quinn, Distinguished Professor of Management,
University of Michigan Business School

Appreciative Inquiry is the philosophy that is allowing us to engage the hearts, minds, and souls of our people—all of our people. Only when we do that, will we achieve breakthrough performance.

—Cindy Frick, VP, Organizational Development and HR Planning,
Roadway Express

[AI is] a process that gets you moving up the success spiral rather than down the failure one. It has a motivating effect helping achieve self-fulfillment rather than getting into a doom and gloom syndrome.

—Rob Treeby, Health, Safety, and Environment Manager, BP AMOCO

I would like to commend you more particularly for your methodology of Appreciative Inquiry and to thank you for introducing it to the United Nations. Without this, it would have been very difficult, perhaps even impossible, to constructively engage so many leaders of business, civil society, and government (for the UN Global Compact Leadership Summit in 2004).

—Kofi Annan, Secretary General, United Nations

We introduced the concept of Appreciative Inquiry into our "Breakthrough Leadership at Roadway" curriculum. Our senior managers have been enthusiastic about using this innovative approach to deal with some of our most pressing issues. The output has been amazing and provides a great map to desirable outcomes.

—Jim Staley, President, Roadway Express

I had the privilege of utilizing an AI methodology with a sales and marketing organization involved in a strategic alliance with a major channel partner. In the two plus years since AI had been introduced to and embraced by the group, a significant transformation has occurred. Morale has improved dramatically, relationships have grown tighter, teamwork has significantly improved—and equally compelling—sales and profitability outpaced the rest of both organizations. A holistic "appreciative approach'" has truly become the way of life for this organization.

—Jim Gustafson, Vice President and General Manager, ELECTRICjob.com

Appreciative Inquiry is helping us be "a breakthrough organization." We started by closing our entire factory and bringing all seven hundred people from the shop floor to the directors together to plan our future. It was a four-day meeting. This year we will use AI to bring one thousand people into the strategic planning and participative redesign process, including all our internal people and representatives of external stakeholders—suppliers, customers and community.

The best in people comes out when you bring the whole system into the room. Wholeness is healthy and that is our purpose at Nutrimental Foods: to produce health-ability. It is exciting, and it pays. After our first large group session profits rose 200 percent and absenteeism, in the next year, dropped 75 percent. AI is about connecting with spirit, self-organization, and self-sustainability, and in the final analysis, human happiness. I wish you could all come and experience our next session!

—Rodrigo Loures, CEO, Nutrimental Foods, Brazil

APPRECIATIVE INQUIRY

APPRECIATIVE INQUIRY
A POSITIVE REVOLUTION
IN CHANGE

DAVID L. COOPERRIDER
& DIANA WHITNEY

BK

Berrett–Koehler Publishers, Inc.
a BK Business book

Berrett-Koehler Publishers, Inc.
1333 Broadway. Suite 1000
Oakland, CA 94612-1921
Tel: 510-817-2277 Fax: 510-817-2278 www.bkconnection.com

Ordering Information

Quantity sales Special discounts are available on quantity purchases by corporations, associations, and others. For details, contact the "Special Sales Department" at the Berrett-Koehler address above.

Individual sales Berrett-Koehler publications are available through most bookstores. They can also be ordered direct from Berrett-Koehler: Tel: (800) 929-2929; Fax (802) 864-7626.

Orders for college textbook/course adoption use Please contact Berrett-Koehler:
Tel: (800) 929-2929; Fax (802) 864-7626.

Distributed to the US trade and internationally by Penguin Random House Publisher Services.

Berrett-Koehler and BK logo are registered trademarks of Berrett-Koehler Publishers, Inc.

Printed in the United States of America

Berrrett-Koehler books are printed on long-lasting acid-free paper. When it is available, we choose paper that has been manufactured by environmentally responsible processes. These may include using trees grown in sustainable forests, incorporating recycled paper, minimizing chlorine in bleaching, or recycling the energy produced at the paper mill.

Library of Congress Cataloging-in-Publication Data

Cooperrider, David L.

   Appreciative Inquiry : a positive revolution in Change / by David L Cooperrider and Diana Whitney.

     p. cm.

Includes index.

ISBN-10: 1-57675-356-5; ISBN-13: 978-1-57675-356-9

    1.   Organizational change. 2. Organizational behavior. I. Whitney, Dianan Kaplin. II. Title.

HD58.8.C6567 2005

658.4'06—dc22   2005048152

First Edition

23 22 21   20 19 18 17 16

Book Design & Production: Jimmie Young • Copy Editing: Susan Pink •
Cover Design: The Visual Group

CONTENTS

Preface

$\cdots\cdots\cdots\cdots\cdots\cdots\cdots\cdots\cdots\cdots\cdots\cdots\cdots\cdots\cdots\cdots\cdots\cdots\cdots\cdots$

Appreciative Inquiry (AI) is a new model of change management, uniquely suited to the values, beliefs, and business challenges facing managers and leaders today. It is a process for large-scale change management that can enable you to engage and inspire your highly diverse and dispersed workforce; to involve customers and other stakeholders in the future of your business; to discover and extend your business strengths and strategic advantages; and to balance outstanding financial returns with heightened societal contributions.

This small book is an introduction to Appreciative Inquiry. It provides a basic overview of the process and principles of AI along with actual stories illustrating how successful businesses have applied AI—and the benefits they have gained as a result. It is not intended to provide a thorough treatment of the subject, nor does it aim to be a how-to book. Instead, this book is written as an invitation, as a starting point into the exciting world of positive organizational change.

We suggest two of our other books for a more through coverage of AI and positive change. *The Appreciative Inquiry Handbook* provides a comprehensive explanation of the subject along with numerous supporting articles and sample materials. *The Power of Appreciative Inquiry* offers a thorough explanation of how to get started and lead an AI initiative.

AI is a process that starts with strengths and, as the stories in this book illustrate, results in dramatic improvements in the triple bottom line: people, profits, and planet. The book tells of how AI has been used to significantly enhance employee engagement, retention, and morale, customer satisfaction, cost competitiveness, revenues and profits, as well as businesses' understanding and abilities to meet the needs of society.

If results such as Nutrimental Food's 200 percent increase in revenues, or Hunter Douglas Window Fashions Division's $3.5 million in savings, or Green Mountain Coffee Roasters acting for the greater good while building exceptional returns and profitability seem extraordinary to you, read this book and discover how and why they are becoming the norm for companies using Appreciative Inquiry.

As thought leaders and pioneers in the growing field of positive change, we have had the good fortune to introduce AI to organizations and communities around the world. Some of the work described in this book in organizations such as Roadway Express, Verizon, British Airways, Green Mountain Coffee Roasters, Hunter Douglas WFD, Nutrimental Foods, the United Nations, and the United Religions Initiative is setting a precedent for the emergence of new, life-affirming, results-oriented practices of positive change management. We are glad that you—by reading this book—have decided to join us in this positive revolution.

David L Cooperrider and Diana Whitney
October 2005

Chapter One

An Invitation to the Positive Revolution in Change

A ppreciative Inquiry (AI) is, as Professor Robert Quinn at University of Michigan has recently written, "creating a positive revolution in the field of organization development and change management."[1] Why? One clue lies in how AI turns the practice of change management inside out. It proposes, quite bluntly, that organizations are not, at their core, problems to be solved. Just the opposite. Every organization was created as a solution designed in its own time to meet a challenge or satisfy a need of society.

Even more fundamentally, organizations are centers of vital connections and life-giving potentials: relationships, partnerships, alliances, and ever-expanding webs of knowledge and action that are capable of harnessing the power of combinations of strengths. Founded upon this lifecentric view of organizations, AI offers a positive, strengths-based approach to organization development and change management.

AI and the New Model of Change Leadership

Management guru Peter Drucker commented in a recent interview, "The task of organizational leadership is to create an alignment of strengths in ways that make a system's weaknesses irrelevant." Could it be, as Drucker implies, that leading change is *all* about strengths? Why would strength connected to strength create positive change? What would it mean to create an entire change methodology around an economy and ecology of strengths? Where would we—as managers, facilitators, and change leaders—start? What might be the steps and stages of positive change? What about unique skills? How could the discovery and fusion of strengths elevate and extend a system's capacity to adapt, learn, and create *upward spirals* of performance, development, and energizing growth?

Indeed, the field of management has always acknowledged that strengths perform and that their very presence, that is, the visible display of strengths, signals some kind of optimal functioning. The principles and practices of Appreciative Inquiry (AI) suggest the idea that collective strengths do more than perform—*they transform*.

At the surface, this sounds obvious and good. But when we pause and take stock of the way contemporary change management is practiced, we see clearly that positive approaches to change are not yet the norm.

Many, for example, were shocked at the results of the largest, most comprehensive survey ever conducted on approaches to managing change. The study concluded that most schools, companies, families and organizations function on an unwritten rule. That rule is to fix what's wrong and let the strengths take care of themselves.

Although the results of this study do not sound like the Peter Drucker quote put into practice, where change is all about strengths, the research conclusion unfortunately rings familiar and true. Companies all too often call for low-morale surveys instead of designing rigorous inquiries into extraordinary moments of high engagement, commitment, and passionate achievement. Managers charter and analyze turnover rates—one report after another—instead of calling for analyses of retention or of *magnetic work environments*, that is, times when people felt so connected to their work, their colleagues, and their organization that the bonds could not be broken.

How pervasive is this deficit-based approach to change, which says change begins with the identification of the most pressing problems, the gaps, and their root causes? Do you recognize it? Okay, try this: Think about the last three projects you've worked on and the last half dozen meetings you've attended. How many of the projects were designed to fix something? How many of the meetings were called to address a problem?

This book puts forth a bold challenge: Could it be that we as a field have reached the end of problem solving as a mode of inquiry capable of inspiring, mobilizing, and sustaining significant human system change? What would happen to our change practices if we began all our work with the positive presumption that organizations, as centers of human relatedness, are alive with infinite constructive capacity?

This book provides a beginning answer in an overview of the newest findings related to the definitions, principles, and practices of Appreciative Inquiry as a model for change leadership. Drawing upon twenty years of practice since AI's birth at the Case Western Reserve University's School of Management, we share stories of the success of positive change—bold and inspiring experiments in businesses and communities around the world.[2] Our hope is that this book will open your hearts and minds to the possibilities of positive change and the many ways that Appreciative Inquiry can help you and your organization achieve your greatest potential in service to a world of peace and prosperity for all.

Approaching Problems From the Other Side

Appreciative Inquiry (AI) begins an adventure. Even in the first steps, one senses an exciting new direction in our language and theories of change—an invitation, as some have declared, to a "positive revolution." The words just quoted *are* strong, but the more we replay the high-wire moments of our five years of work at GTE/Verizon,[3] the more we find ourselves asking the very same kinds of questions that the people of GTE asked their senior executives: "Are you really ready for the momentum that is being generated? This is igniting a grassroots movement . . . it *is* creating an organization in full voice, a center stage for positive revolutionaries!"

Tom White, president of what was then called GTE, Telops (making up 80 percent of GTE's sixty-seven thousand employees), replied with no hesitation: "Yes, and what I see in this meeting are zealots, people with a mission and passion for creating the new GTE. Count me in, I'm your number one recruit, number-one zealot." People cheered.

Fourteen months later, GTE's whole-system change initiative won the ASTD (American Society for Training and Development) award for the best organization change program in the country. This award was based on significant and measurable changes in stock prices, morale survey measures, quality and customer relations, union-management relations, and more. Appreciative inquiry was cited as the "backbone."[4]

To achieve this stunning shift in organizational culture, the team of internal and external change agents asked, "How can we engage the positive potential of all employees toward transforming the company?" The team wanted whatever we did to recognize and invite the positive expression of frontline employee strengths, initiatives, and capabilities. We set a goal of creating a narrative-rich culture with a ratio of five stories of positive performance and success to every negative one as a way of building a vibrant, high-performing, customer-focused culture.

This goal was approached in a number of ways:

■ In year one, more than fifty internal change agents (OD consultants, ER managers, Public Affairs and Corporate Communications staff) received extensive training in Appreciative Inquiry. In addition, Appreciative Inquiry was taught to eight hundred frontline employees.

- Opportunities for sharing good news stories were created. One executive volunteered to be the story center. The stories came into his office, and he sent them out to other groups and departments to share and replicate. Many were published in the company newsletter.

- Storytelling was embedded into many existing processes. For example, the annual President's Leadership award focused on relaying stories about winning employees, their teams, and customer service.

- Open-ended questions were added to the company employee survey, and the ratio of positive to negative comments was tracked.

- An Appreciative Inquiry storybook was created as a teaching tool for all employees.

- Appreciative Inquiry was used to introduce a new partnership model for the unions and for company management.[5]

Based on his experience, Tom White described AI in executive language: "Appreciative Inquiry can get you much better results than seeking out and solving problems. That's an interesting concept for me—and I imagine most of you—because telephone companies are among the best problem solvers in the world. We troubleshoot everything. We concentrate enormous resources on correcting problems that have relatively minor impact on our overall service and performance . . . when used continually and over a long period of time, this approach can lead to a negative culture. If you combine a negative culture with all the challenges we face today, it could be easy to convince ourselves that we have too many problems to overcome—to slip into a paralyzing sense of hopelessness. . . . Don't get me wrong. I'm not advocating mindless happy talk. Appreciative Inquiry is a complex science designed to make things better. We can't ignore problems—we just need to approach them from the other side."[6]

Are you ready for a positive approach to change? Are you tired of the same old discussions of what's not working, how hard it is to overcome, and who's to blame? Do you have hopes and dreams for your organization? Would you like to see engagement, commitment, and enthusiasm rise along with revenues and profits? Are you searching for a process to open communication, unleash human potential, and create a truly learning organization? If your answer to any of these questions is yes, you are ready to accept the invitation to the positive revolution, to embrace Appreciative Inquiry, and to benefit from a positive approach to change management.

Chapter Two

What is Appreciative Inquiry?

Ap-pre'ci-ate, v., 1. Valuing; the act of recognizing the best in people or the world around us; affirming past and present strengths, successes, and potentials; to perceive those things that give life (health, vitality, excellence) to living systems. 2. To increase in value, e.g., the economy has appreciated in value. Synonyms: value, prize, esteem, and honor.

In-quire', v., 1. The act of exploration and discovery. 2. To ask questions; to be open to seeing new potentials and possibilities. Synonyms: discover, search, systematically explore, and study.

T he term AI has been described in a myriad of ways: as a radically affirmative approach to change that completely lets go of problem-based management and in so doing vitally transforms strategic planning, survey methods, culture change, merger integration methods . . . measurement systems;[7] as a paradigm of conscious evolution geared for the realities of the new century;[8] as the most important advance in action research in the past decade;[9] as offspring and heir to Maslow's vision of a positive social science;[10] and as a methodology that takes the idea of the social construction of reality to its positive extreme, especially with its emphasis on metaphor and narrative, relational ways of knowing, on language, and on its potential as a source of generative theory.[11]

Although AI can be described in many ways—as a philosophy and methodology for change leadership—here is a practice-oriented definition:

> Appreciative Inquiry is the cooperative, coevolutionary search for the best in people, their organizations, and the world around them. It involves systematic discovery of what gives life to an organization or a community when it is most effective and most capable in economic, ecological, and human terms.

> In AI, intervention gives way to inquiry, imagination, and innovation. Instead of negation, criticism, and spiraling diagnosis, there is discovery, dream, and design. AI involves the art and practice of asking unconditionally positive questions that strengthen a system's capacity to apprehend, anticipate, and heighten positive potential. Through mass mobilized inquiry, hundreds and even thousands of people can be involved in cocreating their collective future.

> AI assumes that every organization and community has many untapped and rich accounts of the positive—what people talk about as past, present, and future capacities, or the positive core. AI links the knowledge and energy of this core directly to an organization or a community's change agenda, and changes never thought possible are suddenly and democratically mobilized.

The Positive Core

The *positive core* of organizational life is one of the greatest and largely unrecognized resources in the field of change management today. We are clearly in our infancy when it comes to tools for working with the positive core, talking about it, and designing our systems in synergistic alignment with it. But one thing is evident and clear as we reflect on the most important things we have learned with AI:

Human systems grow in the direction of what they persistently ask questions about, and this propensity is strongest and most sustainable when the means and ends of inquiry are positively correlated. The single most important action a group can take to liberate the human spirit and consciously construct a better future is to make the positive core the common and explicit property of all.

Table 1 shows the diverse set of assets, strengths, and resources that, when discussed, broadly constitute an organization or a community's positive core. Conversations about the positive core bring it to life, give it meaning and enable an organization's members and stakeholders to share best practices.

Achievements	Vital traditions
Strategic opportunities	Lived values
Product strengths	Positive macrotrends
Technical assets	Social capital
Breakthrough innovations	Collective spirit
Elevated thoughts	Embedded knowledge
Best business practices	Financial assets
Positive emotions	Visions of positive futures
Organization wisdom	Alliances and partnerships
Core competencies	Value chain strengths
Visions of possibility	Strategic advantages
Leadership capabilities	Relational resources
Product pipeline	Customer loyalty

Table I The Positive Core of Organizational Life

In the process of inquiry into its positive core, an organization enhances its collective wisdom, builds energy and resiliency to change, and extends its capacity to achieve extraordinary results. We call this process mapping the *positive core*. Figures 1 and 2 are photos of two positive *core maps*: the creative renderings that emerge when a group of people discover and share stories of their most positive experiences and best practices.

Nurses at DuBois Regional Medical Center drew Figure 1-a "positive core" mural for "Building Capacity for Better Work and Better Care ," a HRSA (Health Resources and Services Administration) funded project in 6 hospitals in PA. Donna Sullivan Havens, PhD, RN, The University of North Carolina at Chapel Hill School of Nursing, led the project working with Susan O. Wood, Corporation for Positive Change.

Figure 1 A positive core mural

Figure 2 A map of the positive core of strengths.

The positive core map in Figure 2 was created by two hundred people during a two-day AI summit led by Jim Ludema and Diana Whitney to enhance excellence in customer service at Santa Ana Star Casino. One-on-one interviews were conducted, and then small groups of people shared stories from their interviews and identified the elements of the organization's positive core shown here on the stars in Figure 2.

A Working Definition of Positive Change

In everything it does, AI deliberately seeks to work from accounts of the positive core. This shift from problem analysis to positive core analysis is at the heart of positive change.

In the old paradigm, change begins with a clear definition of the problem. Problem-solving approaches to change

■ Are painfully slow, always asking people to look backward to yesterday's causes

■ Rarely result in new vision

■ Are notorious for generating defensiveness

With AI, change begins with a rigorous, organization-wide discovery and analysis of the positive core, what we sometimes call a root cause of success analysis. Figure 3 illustrates the shift from a problem-solving approach to change management to an AI approach to positive change management.

Positive change can be defined as follows:

Any form of organization change, redesign, or planning that begins with a comprehensive inquiry, analysis, and dialogue· of an organization's positive core, that involves multiple stakeholders, and then links this knowledge to the organization's strategic change agenda and priorities.

Organizations around the world have made the shift from problem solving to AI to create positive change for a range of strategic agendas including the following: building partnerships and alliances; transforming corporate culture; strategic planning; reducing product development time; enhancing employee retention and morale; and productivity, quality, and financial improvement.

In the spring of 2003, the Denver Office of Finance initiated a citywide inquiry to discover and disseminate financial best practices and to identify revenue-generating opportunities across the city. This initiative was explicitly targeted to save $70 million. To build a grassroots commitment to cost savings, a team of two hundred people were trained and conducted six hundred face-to-face interviews with city employees, local businesses, and community members. They then came together for a one-day AI summit to articulate best practices, envision a stable financial future, and design and initiate individual department-level and cross-agency cost-saving and revenue-generating projects. Margaret Brown, Manager of Budget and Finance, City and County of Denver, and project consultants Lynn Pollard and Amanda Trosten-Bloom reported the following financial results:

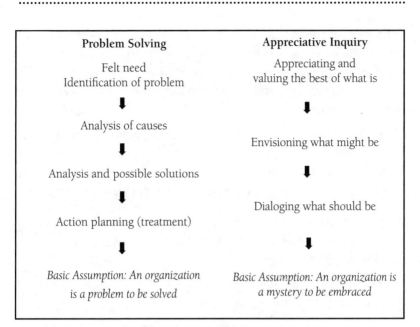

Problem Solving	Appreciative Inquiry
Felt need Identification of problem	Appreciating and valuing the best of what is
↓	↓
Analysis of causes	
↓	Envisioning what might be
Analysis and possible solutions	↓
↓	
Action planning (treatment)	Dialoging what should be
↓	↓
Basic Assumption: An organization *is a problem to be solved*	*Basic Assumption: An organization is* *a mystery to be embraced*

Figure 3 From problem solving to appreciative inquiry.

- Extensive consolidation of services reduced duplicated services and led to cost savings. For example, a downsizing of fleet services resulted in a $370,000 savings.

- Relocation and consolidation of agency offices from leased space to city-owned space. Among the many savings this afforded was a reduced cost for building security, saving $358,000 per year.

- Development of a new incentive retirement program. This program saved $1.5 million per year.

In addition, employee morale, commitment to cost savings, and the ongoing discovery of innovative revenue-generating ideas were elevated through the use of AI. Voluntary suggestions for improved fiscal management continue at a rate of up to fifty emails per day. Many of the suggestions reflect the new approach: collaborative and consolidated services, which reduce costs and provide a better quality of service to the citizens of Denver.

Positive change, like what was experienced in Denver, begins with an inquiry into the positive core—what works well when the organization or community is at its best. AI is a process for engaging an entire organization and its stakeholders in creating a future that works for everyone.

At the heart of AI is the *appreciative interview*, a one-on-one dialogue among organization members and stakeholders using questions related to: highpoint experiences, valuing, and what gives life to the organization at its best. Questions such as the following are asked:

■ Describe a time in your organization that you consider a highpoint experience, a time when you were most engaged and felt alive and vibrant.

■ Without being modest, tell me what it is that you most value about yourself, your work, and your organization.

■ What are the core factors that give life to your organization when it is at its best?

■ Imagine your organization ten years from now, when everything is just as you always wished it could be. What is different? How have you contributed to this dream organization?

Answers to questions like these and the stories they generate are shared throughout the organization, resulting in new, more compelling images of the organization and its future.

Is your organization's positive core the implicit property of all? How often do you engage the members of your organization in dialogue about your positive core? Do you start meetings with a review of accomplishments? Do you study the causes of your successes? Imagine a day of sharing stories about what makes your company great.

Chapter Three

The Appreciative Inquiry 4-D Cycle

··

Appreciative Inquiry is a narrative-based process of positive change. It is a cycle of activity that starts by engaging all members of an organization or community in a broad set of interviews and deep dialogue about strengths, resources, and capabilities. It then moves people through a series of activities focused on envisioning bold possibilities and lifting up the most lifecentric dreams for the future. From there, it asks people to discuss and craft propositions that will guide their future together. And finally, it involves the formation of teams to carry out the work needed to realize the new dream and designs for the future. This process is called the AI 4-D cycle. This chapter gives you a brief overview of the 4-D cycle and how it gets started.

Overview of the 4-D Cycle

The AI cycle can be as rapid and informal as a conversation with a friend or a colleague, or as formal as an organization-wide process involving every stakeholder group. Although AI has no formula, the change efforts of most organizations flow through the 4-D cycle shown in Figure 4. Each AI process is homegrown, designed to meet the unique challenges of the organization and industry involved.

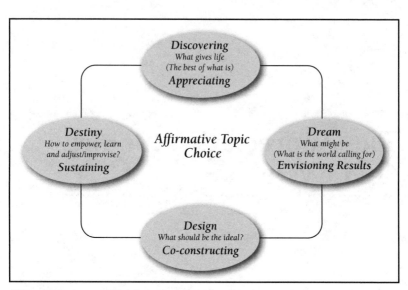

Figure 4 Appreciative Inquiry 4-D cycle.

The four key phases of an AI process, illustrated in Figure 4, are as follows:

■ **Discovery**: Mobilizing the whole system by engaging all stakeholders in the articulation of strengths and best practices. Identifying "The best of what has been and what is."

■ **Dream**: Creating a clear results-oriented vision in relation to discovered potential and in relation to questions of higher purpose, such as, "What is the world calling us to become?"

■ **Design**: Creating possibility propositions of the ideal organization, articulating an organization design that people feel is capable of drawing upon and magnifying the positive core to realize the newly expressed dream.

■ **Destiny**: Strengthening the affirmative capability[12] of the whole system, enabling it to build hope and sustain momentum for ongoing positive change and high performance.

At the center of the cycle is *affirmative topic choice*. It is the starting point and the most strategic aspect of any AI process. Selecting affirmative topics is an opportunity for members of an organization to set a strategic course for the future. AI topics become an organization's agenda for learning, knowledge sharing, and action. The topics selected set the stage for the 4-D process that follows. They get written into questions that are the basis for discovery interviews. They serve as seeds for the dreams phrase and as arenas for crafting design propositions and taking action in the destiny phase.

Each application of AI is different. The purpose or strategic change agenda for the AI initiative creates a context for the selection of topics. Within that context, members of the organization choose topics to move the organization in a direction they find desirable. For example, Hunter Douglas has used AI for several change initiatives over the past eight years. The purpose of the first change initiative was companywide cultural transformation. A team of one hundred employees selected topics to uncover and leverage their strengths. They chose five general topics as the focus of their inquiry: people, education, communication, recognition, and teamwork. In their second application of Appreciative Inquiry, more specific topics were chosen. The focus of the second companywide effort was strategic planning, and the inquiry topics chosen were: culture as competitive advantage, strategic business opportunities, growth through innovation, and strategic leadership. As this illustrates, in each application of AI, topics are chosen to lead the organization toward its desired future.

The process of selecting affirmative topics:

- Involves a cross section of people from throughout the organization

- Grows out of preliminary interviews into the organization at its best

- Challenges people to reframe deficit issues into affirmative topics for inquiry.

In the next section, we consider the way the process of topic choice unfolded at British Airways, NA.

Passion for Service: Getting Started with AI at British Airways

After two years of significant organizational changes, including the addition of stations, new alliances, technology upgrades, leadership transitions, and facility refurbishing, David Erich, V.P. of Customer Service for British Airways NA realized his job had just begun. He felt it was time to engage employees in making changes that would directly enhance both their satisfaction and their capacity to provide the outstanding customer service for which British Airways is known worldwide.

He and his team began a search for a process that would make a positive difference in lagging employee survey scores while revitalizing the British Airways culture of passion for service. In May 1999, one British Airways team learned about Appreciative Inquiry through an e-mail exchange with a colleague. By August of the same year, they had begun a whole-system process using Appreciative Inquiry to transform the organization's culture; or as Deal and Kennedy put it, "the way we do things around here."[13] Much was being accomplished throughout the British Airways Customer Service system. The dilemma was one of communication. From station to station, people were not identifying, sharing, or replicating best practices. The organization's collective wisdom was like an underground well, full of life-giving potential waiting to be drawn upon and put to good use. Appreciative Inquiry seemed like a viable way to identify and spread best practices across the twenty-two British Airways stations in North America.

The introduction of Appreciative Inquiry to the organization and the decision to proceed with the whole-system process were iterative and ultimately involved more than fifty people. A conference call with a few executives led to a one-day briefing for a small group of line managers and organization development professionals. They sensed merit in Appreciative Inquiry's positive, high-participation approach to organization transformation, but wanted to be certain it would "fly" at British Airways. After speaking with colleagues at other organizations involved with Appreciative Inquiry, such as Hunter Douglas and GTE/Verizon, they decided to take the next step.

Forty people from all levels, locations, and functions of the organization were invited to attend a two-day core team meeting. They would be the group to decide whether or not to bring Appreciative Inquiry into the organization. If they decided to go forward, their work would serve as the foundation for the whole-system inquiry that would follow.

The two days included an overview of the principles and practices of Appreciative Inquiry. As a primary means of learning how Appreciative Inquiry works, the core team went through the process of selecting affirmative topics and drafting interview questions. They conducted practice interviews and shared stories of best practices. The two days were a rich sharing of organizational wisdom as well as an opportunity to learn about Appreciative Inquiry as a positive approach to work, leadership, and change management.

Selecting affirmative topics for inquiry

Several hours into the core team meeting, as the group of forty was selecting affirmative inquiry topics, one participant raised a question about the applicability of Appreciative Inquiry. She commented, "I see how Appreciative Inquiry can make a big difference with people-related issues, but can it be used for technical issues?" Sensing that this was not merely a theoretical question and that she had a very specific technical issue in mind, we asked her to share the technical issue she was hoping Appreciative Inquiry might help. She said succinctly, "Baggage." At that point, everyone in the room uttered a great sigh of relief. The issue they considered paramount to the well-being of their business was now in the conversation.

Being relatively new to the airline industry, we asked the group to fill us in, to tell us about the baggage issue. With great energy, emphasis, and sometimes frustration, they explained that when a customer's baggage does not arrive on the same flight as the customer, the costs to British Airways rise—in time, money, and goodwill. And of course, they shared stories of the wedding dress that didn't make it to the wedding on time and had to be replaced at British Airways' expense; camping gear that didn't get to the Grand Canyon until the week's vacation was over; as well as the daily disturbances of luggage not making it through its transfer from Heathrow to Gatwick in time for connecting flights.

We knew we were in the midst of people who care for their customers when one customer service agent said, "This is not how we like to do things at British Airways. It's not what our customers expect, and it doesn't make us proud of what we do or who we are. What can we do about it?"

We paraphrased their stories to demonstrate our understanding of their concerns for the issue. Then we repeated the Appreciative Inquiry principle that leads to powerful, strategic affirmative topics, "Given that organizations move in the direction of what they study, what is it that you want more of in British Airways? In this case, we know you do not want more lost or delayed baggage. But what do you want more of?"

The groups' response came too quickly and unanimously to be anything other than the organization's habitual response to the situation. Several people, almost simultaneously, said, "Better service recovery." We paused to reflect upon the most helpful way to reply, and then said, "Let me see if I have this right. It's okay to lose a customers' baggage as long as you recover it promptly?" The group got the point immediately and said "No, no, it's not okay."

Again we asked, "So what do you want more of? What affirmative topic would move this organization in the direction you want to see it go?" Small groups talked for about twenty minutes and then we shared ideas. Among the many innovative ideas was the topic they called exceptional arrival experience. One group was emphatic that what they wanted more of was for all British Airways customers to have an exceptional arrival experience. When the entire group discussed this potential topic, there was a great deal of consensus. One person said how much more like British Airways at its best it would be if customer service agents were focused on providing exceptional arrival experiences rather than worrying about lost baggage. Exceptional arrival experience was selected along with happiness at work, continuous people development, and harmony among work groups as the four affirmative topics for an organization-wide inquiry.

This is a classic example of the power of topic choice. Affirmative topics, always homegrown, can be about anything that the people of an organization feel gives life to the system. As a general rule, most projects have between three and five topics. Words such as empowerment, innovation, sense of ownership, commitment, integrity, ecological consciousness, and pride are often articulated as worthy of study. Topics can be about anything an organization feels to be strategically and humanly important. As the British Airways story illustrates, AI topics can be on technical processes, financial efficiencies, human issues, market opportunities, social responsibilities, or anything else. In each case of topic choice, the same premise is firmly posited: Human systems grow in the direction of their deepest and most frequent inquiries.

What is it that you want more of in your organization? Imagine hundreds of people conducting interviews and dialogues on this strategic topic. What might they learn and what changes would spontaneously begin to happen?

Deciding to go forward

Toward the end of the two-day British Airways meeting, we posed two questions: "Should British Airways Customer Service go forward with Appreciative Inquiry?" and "What will it take to ensure success?" By this time in the meeting, the answer to the first question was a unanimous yes. As a result, the group of Appreciative Inquiry champions had expanded from a small group of executives in New York to an enthusiastic group of fifty or so people throughout North America. A most dramatic testimonial and call for commitment came from an employee with less than a year to retirement. She took the microphone and won the hearts of her colleagues when she shared her view of what Appreciative Inquiry could do for the company.

> "I came to this meeting because I was so frustrated with what has happened around here in the past few years. I have worked here for twenty-five years and I love this company, but it's not the same as it used to be. And it's not as good. We've become so cynical and negative. I am retiring in less than a year and before these two days I couldn't wait to get out. Now, after this meeting, I feel hopeful again. I want to be involved with Appreciative Inquiry so when I retire I will be proud of the company. With this process, we can bring back the old feelings by learning from each other and by doing new things. It will take all of us and we will have to work together, but we can do it. And we have to do it; otherwise things will just get worse around here. I am going back to my station and telling everyone about what I learned. And next week, I will interview my manager. That's how I'll start the ball rolling. What will you do?"

After several more passion-filled calls for action by various core team members, it was time to answer the question, "What will it take for this initiative to succeed?" The group collectively and emphatically agreed upon two essential factors for success: management commitment and the involvement of the entire workforce. It was clearly suggested that without either of these, the effort would be "same old, same old" and would not make a bit of difference. For Appreciative Inquiry to be a viable philosophy and tool to revitalize the culture of passion for service, whole-system involvement was needed. Everyone, at all levels throughout the entire organization, had to be invited to participate in such a way as to rally their support and involvement.

The core team agreed to shepherd the process. They volunteered to support the effort by signing up for a series of follow-on roles that included conducting interviews, naming and branding the initiative, speaking to groups about AI, writing articles or being interviewed for in-house communications, and serving as their station AI coordinator.

The next step was to ensure that the two articulated success factors were realized.

A steering team was formed to address these issues and to serve as designers, champions, and supporters of the overall process. Made up of line managers, executives, people and organization development managers, communication consultants, and the Appreciative Inquiry consultant, the team's high performance served as a benchmark for the entire initiative.

A one-day management briefing was held, before which several core team members conducted interviews with their own managers using the draft interview guide. They explained to their managers what to expect when they attended the Appreciative Inquiry briefing. Already we had turned power relations for many upside down. During their briefing, the managers heard about Appreciative Inquiry from the consultant, they heard about the proposed British Airways process now called "The Power of Two," and they heard from a subgroup of the core team who spoke about their enthusiasm for AI and the potential it held for British Airways. By the end of this meeting, AI was off and flying at British Airways, NA.

Chapter Four

The 4-D Cycle in Action

N o two Appreciative Inquiry processes are alike. Each is designed to address a unique strategic challenge faced by the organization or industry. Each is designed to optimize participation among stakeholders. This means that the four D's of AI—discovery, dream, design, and destiny—can take many forms of expression. In this chapter, we provide a further explanation of each of the four D's along with an example of how the AI process has been carried out in one organization.

The First D, Discovery

The core discovery task is disclosing positive capacity. AI invites systemwide dialogue and learning through a process of appreciative interviewing. When asked how many people should be interviewed or who should do the interviews, we increasingly say "everyone" because, in the process, people reclaim their ability to admire, be surprised, be inspired, and appreciate the best in others and in their organization.

At the heart of discovery is the *appreciative interview*. The uniqueness and power of an AI interview stem from its fundamentally affirmative focus. What distinguishes AI at this phase is that every question is positive. During appreciative interviews, people uncover what gives life to their organization, department, or community when at its best. They discover personal and organizational highpoints, what people value, and how they hope and wish to enhance their organization's social, economic, and environmental vitality.

During the discovery phase, people throughout a system connect to study examples of what makes them their best, to analyze and map their positive core, and to investigate their root causes of success. As they connect, they build relationships, organizational wisdom expands, useful and innovative knowledge is shared, and hope grows. AI provides a practical way to ignite this spirit of inquiry on an organization-wide basis. Consider the following example.

At Leadshare, a big eight accounting firm in Canada, AI was used for the executive succession of a legendary managing partner. The retiring managing partner seized the opportunity to leave a living legacy by engaging all four hundred partners in the process. An extensive interview protocol was designed (each interview averaged about two hours) that focused on affirmative topics such as innovation, equality, partnership, speed to market, and valuing diversity (a key success factor in this Canadian business). All four hundred partners were interviewed. The interviews were conducted by thirty junior partners as part of their leadership development program. A powerful and instant intergenerational connection was made, and organizational history came alive in face-to-face stories. People began to relate to their history in a new way. Like a good poem filled with endless interpretive meaning, people at Leadshare ascended into their history as a reservoir of positive possibility. At the next partners meeting, the material was showcased and coupled to the future. One participant commented, "This strategic planning process became one of the best the partners could ever remember."

From Discovery to Dream

An artist's imagination is kindled not by searching for what is wrong with this picture but by being inspired by those things worth valuing.

Appreciation draws our eye toward life, stirs our feelings, sets in motion our curiosity, and inspires the envisioning mind.

"The purpose of the dream phase of AI," according to Ludema et al., "is to engage the whole system in moving beyond the status quo to envision valued and vital futures. It is an invitation to people to lift their sights, exercise their imagination, and discuss what their organization could look like if it were fully aligned around its strengths and aspirations."[14] During the dream phase, interview stories and insights get put to constructive use. Stories, analysis, and maps of the positive core serve as essential resources for the visioning stage of AI.

At Hunter Douglas WFD, mapping the positive core was followed by reflection on the question, "What is the implication of this map of the positive core for the future of our business?" The resulting discussion was energizing and surprising. One member of the organization remarked, "Our competencies are not in windows, as we have thought for years. They are in our technologies. If we apply our technologies to new areas, we can create new products and new businesses." And that is exactly what they did. The strategic plan that came out of this meeting called for the development of a new, nonwindow product within five years. They excelled, and within three years they had designed and prototyped the new product (a ceiling tile) and created a business unit that successfully led them into new markets.

The dream phase calls for people to listen carefully to moments of organizational life at its best and to share images of their hopes and dreams for their collective future. As possibilities for the future are articulated and enacted they come to life.

Before their first strategic planning session using Appreciative Inquiry, Nutrimental Foods of Brazil closed down the plant for a full day to bring all seven hundred employees together for a day of discovery into the factors and forces that have given life to the system when it had been most effective, most alive, and most successful as a producer of high-quality health foods. With cheers and good wishes, a smaller group of one hundred fifty stakeholders—employees from all levels, suppliers, distributors, community leaders, financiers, and customers—went into a four-day strategy session to articulate a new and bold corporate dream. With the stories from the day before in mind, people were asked to dream: "What is the world calling us to become? What are those things about us that no matter how much we change, we want to continue in our new and different future? Let's assume that tonight, while we were all asleep, a miracle occurred in which Nutrimental became exactly as we would like it to be—all its best qualities magnified, extended, and multiplied. . . . We wake up and it is now 2005. . . . As you come into Nutrimental today, what do you see that is different, and how do you know?"

After four days of appreciative analysis, planning, and articulation of three new strategic business directions, the organization launched into the future with focus, solidarity, and confidence. Six months later, record bottom-line figures of millions of dollars are recorded; profits are up 200 percent. Co-CEOs Rodrigo Loures and Arthur Lemme Netto attribute the dramatic results to two things: bringing the whole system into the planning process, and realizing that organizations are in fact "centers of human relatedness which thrive when there is an appreciative eye—when people see the best in one another, when they can dialogue their dreams and ultimate concerns in affirming ways, and when they are connected in full voice to create not just new worlds but better worlds."

That was 1997. Since then, Loures has used Appreciative Inquiry annually as the process to organize and facilitate whole-system strategic planning, as well as for the founding of an innovative leadership institute to develop appreciative leadership capacity throughout Brazil.

Design for Organizing into the Future

After the strategic focus, or dream, is articulated (a vision of a better world, a powerful purpose, or a compelling statement of strategic intent), attention turns to creating the ideal organization, the social architecture or actual design of the system in relation to its world.

When inspired by a great dream, we have yet to find an organization that did not feel compelled to design something new and necessary.

In Zimbabwe, we worked with a partner organization of Save the Children. It was fascinating to observe how the natural redesign of the organization in terms of structures and systems occurred after broad agreement was reached on a powerful dream. The articulated image of the future was simple: "Every person in Zimbabwe shall have access to clean water within five years." This large dream demanded a large design shift: away from traditional hierarchy to a new form of organization based on a network of alliances or partnerships.

One aspect differentiating Appreciative Inquiry from other visioning or planning methodologies is that images of the future emerge out of *grounded* examples from an organization's positive past. Good news stories are used to craft *possibility propositions* that bridge the best of what is with collective aspiration of what might be.

During the design phase of AI, people are invited to challenge the status quo as well as the common assumptions underlying the design of their organization. People are encouraged to wonder beyond the data with the essential question being, "What would our organization look like if it were designed in every way possible to maximize the qualities of the positive core and enable the accelerated realization of our dreams?"

Here is an example of a possibility proposition, one of about twenty organization design statements that were created at DIA Corporation, a rapidly growing distributor of consumer products. At the time it was written, this proposition was radical. Today it is modus operandi at the corporation:

> DIA is a learning organization that fosters the cross-fertilization of ideas, minimizes the building of empires, harnesses the synergy of group cooperation, and cultivates the pride of being a valued member of one outstanding corporation. DIA accelerates its learning through an annual strategic planning conference that involves all five hundred people in the firm as well as key partners and stakeholders. As a setting for

strategic learning, teams present their benchmarking studies of other organizations deemed leaders in their class. Other teams present an annual appreciative analysis of DIA, and together these databases of success stories (internal and external) help set the stage for DIA's strategic future planning.

Appreciative Inquiry leads to the design of *appreciative organizations*,[15] capable of supporting stakeholders in the realization of the triple bottom line: people, profits, and planet. The transformation of existing organizations into appreciative organizations and the creation of innovative organizations to meet the needs of the twenty-first century follow a similar path through the 4-D cycle, but each requires a slightly different focus at each phase. This is illustrated in Table 2.

	Transforming Existing Organizations	**Creating Appreciative Organizations**
Discovery	• Inquiry into the positive core • Aligning strengths for competitive advantage • Sharing best practices to enhance effectiveness and efficiency	• Inquiry into the call and capacities to create a new organization • Uncovering multiple and diverse stakeholder strengths • Aligning strengths for collective potential
Dream	• Images of a better world • Strategic vision of the organization serving society	• Images of a better world • Engaging large numbers of stakeholders in creating a compelling shared vision and values
Design	• Articulating organizational values • Crafting provocative propositions and organizing principles	• Crafting a clear purpose and set of organizing principles • Crafting a charter of relationships, roles, and responsibilities
Destiny	• Acting to realize the dream in alignment with the principles	• Living the purpose, principles, and charter • Continuous organizational innovation in alignment with the vision and values

Table 2 The AI Process for Creating Appreciative Organizations

In the past decade, organizations such as Hunter Douglas, Nutrimental, Green Mountain Coffee Roasters, DIA, Roadway Express, and the U.S. Navy have transformed their organizational cultures and designs to reflect a commitment to be an appreciative organization. In the same timeframe, several bold innovations have used Appreciative Inquiry in the creation of global organizations. The Mountain Forum, a global organization dedicated to the preservation of mountain environments and cultures worldwide, is one. The United Religions Initiative (URI), a global organization serving peace among religions and on the planet is another. The URI story is one of great conviction, collaboration, and compassion. We have had the honor of being a part of its creation and continue to serve as advisors to the Executive Director and Global Council.

The United Religions Initiative (URI): Design of a Global Community

The story of the creation of the URI is about the birth of a vision and about a bishop who invited the whole world to join him on an inconceivable quest to make that vision real. It is also the story of Appreciative Inquiry's potential as an inclusive methodology and philosophy of large-scale citizen engagement that holds people in high regard and invites them to make a difference through the alignment of strengths.

At the United Nation's fiftieth anniversary celebration in 1995, Bishop Swing, the Episcopal Bishop for the Archdiocese of California, challenged the moral responsibility of religious leaders around the world and called for a *United Religions*, an organization that could be to the world of religions what the United Nations is to nation-states.

Why didn't it already exist? Detractors pointed to twenty other "failed" attempts to create something like it, tracing back more than one hundred years to the first effort in Chicago at the historic September 11, 1893 meeting of the Parliament of the World's Religions.

Bishop Swing and his wife traveled the world to meet with religious leaders of many faiths and share the idea of a UR. They listened to ideas, support, concerns, and ways to include people of all faiths, religions, and traditions. In 1997, he created an interfaith Board of Directors in San Francisco and invited them to create a vibrant, worldwide, interfaith organization dedicated to peace.

In its early vision, the UR would be a bridge-building organization, not a religion, just as the UN is not one nation state but many in dialogue about the well being of the world. He dreamed of an organization of the scope and stature of the UN but uniquely designed to reflect the values of spiritual, religious, and indigenous people of the world.

The Appreciative Inquiry team conceptualized and set in motion a five-year process of AI planning that involved annual large-group global summits at Stanford University in combination with a series of regional, locally rooted summits in between. We partnered with the URI staff and collaboratively guided the global process of dialogue and multistakeholder planning that created a charter and a twenty-first century organizational design modeled in part on work with Dee Hock.[16]

Then, on June 26 2000, the global charter was signed and webcast to the world from Carnegie Music Hall. It included the URI's purpose:

> To promote enduring daily interfaith cooperation, to end religiously motivated violence, and to create cultures of peace, justice, and healing for the Earth and all living beings.

Even then, AI was recognized as having played a significant role in enabling dialogue among the highly diverse group of world religious, spiritual, and indigenous leaders committed to the creation of the URI. As Charles Gibbs, the URI Executive Director, wrote, "AI led a growing global community on its trust walk of cocreation. It opened the door for hundreds and eventually thousands of people to join in an unprecedented act of global cooperation. . . . it is an organization development methodology that is changing human history . . . it is a portal through which one of the most extraordinary resources on earth, the ingenuity and resourcefulness of the human spirit, is tapped."[17]

Following is some of what was accomplished using AI:

- **The development and actualization of a worldwide process of engagement**. More than twenty-five thousand people were directly involved in AI summits, interviews, and conferences providing input to the purpose, principles, and charter.

- **The articulation of a visionary charter for the URI**. This charter includes a shared purpose, constitutional principles, and an internationally recognized set of bylaws.

- **The development of an organizational design of cooperation circles**. These are inclusive, self-organizing, and regionally and globally connected.

- **The formation of a global council**. The council was selected by and made up of members of the URI's cooperation circles, with legal mechanisms designed to ensure social inclusion and vibrant diversity.

- **The construction of an electronic communications architecture**. The web site links the cooperation circles and provides a portal for the world into powerful peace-building resources;

- **The writing of a global agenda for action**. The agenda covers the areas of conflict resolution, environmental restoration, economic development, and creating public awareness of the strengths and rich resources of wisdom from all the world's religious and spiritual traditions.

Today, ten years later, there is a strong, new global organization called the United Religions Initiative (URI)[18] with more than two hundred seventy cooperation circles in fifty-seven countries, several multiple cooperation circles linking three or more like-minded cooperation circles, and an actively growing network of peace builders. The URI celebrated its fifth anniversary in Seoul, Korea, June 26, 2005 (also the fifty-fifth anniversary of the UN) with the inauguration of and transition to its newly elected Global Council.

The design of the URI, like that of other appreciative organizations, is based on principles. Rather than the adage "form follows function," we say that "form follows principle." This allows local units to organize in any way they see fit as long as they adhere to and are congruent with the purpose and principles of the entire organization.

Our work with Dee Hock, the visionary founder and CEO of VISA Corporation, to design the URI gave us insights into how to move pragmatically from centralized command and control organizational designs to truly postbureaucratic designs that distribute power and liberate human energy. If General Motors once defined the shape of the old model of organizing, perhaps Dee's chaordic organization—the combination of chaos and order in ways that enable infinite variety to self organize—is a foreshadowing of an emerging prototype for a new generation of appreciative organizations.

Realizing Destiny

Of all the creatures of earth, said William James in 1902, only human beings can change their pattern. "Man alone is the architect of his destiny."

In our early years of AI work, we called the fourth D delivery, not destiny. We emphasized action planning, developing implementation strategies, and dealing with conventional challenges of sustainability. But the word *delivery* simply did not go far enough. What we discovered working with companies such as GTE, Hunter Douglas, and Nutrimental was that momentum for change and long-term sustainability *increased the more we abandoned delivery ideas of action planning, monitoring progress, and building implementation strategies.* What we did instead, in several of the most exciting cases, was to focus on giving AI away to everyone and then stepping back and letting the transformation emerge. Our experience suggests that organizational change needs to look a lot more like an inspired movement than a neatly packaged or engineered product. Dan Young, the head of Organization Development at GTE, and his colleagues Jean Moore and Maureen Garrison called it "organizing for change from the grassroots of the frontline." Call it the path of positive protest or a strategy for positive subversion. Whatever it is called, it is virtually unstoppable once it is up and running.

What is needed, as the destiny phase of AI indicates, are the network-like structures that liberate not only the daily search into qualities and elements of an organization's positive core but the establishment of a convergence zone for people to empower one another—to connect, cooperate, and cocreate. Changes never thought possible are suddenly and democratically mobilized when people constructively appropriate the power of the positive core and simply *let go* of negative accounts.

Chapter Five

Applying the 4-D Cycle

M any different approaches to applying the 4-D cycle are emerging. From mass mobilizing interviews across an entire city, to small groups of people interviewing colleagues within their company and then benchmarking other best practices companies, to face-to-face interfaith dialogue among hundreds of religious leaders gathered from around the world, each application liberates the power of inquiry, builds relationships, and unleashes learning. In *The Power of Appreciative Inquiry*, Diana Whitney and Amanda Trosten-Bloom outline multiple forms of engagement that have been used by consultants around the globe for applying Appreciative Inquiry.[19] Two of the most often used and successful ways to apply AI are whole-system inquiry[20] and the AI Summit.[21] This chapter offers a brief overview and an illustrative story of both.

Whole-System Inquiry

In a whole-system inquiry, all stakeholders—employees, customers, vendors, and interested community members—participate in the process. During the discovery phase, they are interviewed and may even conduct interviews with one another. In the later phases of dream, design, and destiny, small groups are gathered to share stories and best practices, to envision their collective future, and to launch innovation teams or other improvisational initiatives.

In the case of British Airways' Customer Service, all twelve hundred employees in North America were given the opportunity to be interviewed. About one thousand volunteered. Ten percent of the workforce at each of twenty-two locations were trained as interviewers. They conducted interviews over a six-month time frame, summarized their findings, and held meetings to share stories, innovations, and best practices in their local stations. Three months later, one hundred fifty people, representatives from each station, gathered to share across units and to dream and design. At that time, volunteer innovation teams were formed to spread throughout the entire organization the best practices related to each of the four affirmative topics. This whole-system inquiry involving every employee in the system resulted in significant improvements as measured by the annual employee survey.

The AI Summit

Among the most exciting applications of Appreciative Inquiry is the AI Summit.[22] The AI Summit is a large-scale meeting process that focuses on discovering and developing an organization's positive core and designing it into strategic business processes, such as marketing; customer service; leadership and human resource development; and new product development. Participation is diverse and includes all the organization's stakeholders. A AI Summit is generally four days long and involves fifty to two thousand people or more. The AI Summit is a modality that often results in home runs and strong relational ties that enable ongoing and sustainable innovation, as the following story of Roadway Express illustrates.

Although each AI Summit is unique, successful AI Summits have some common aspects. The four days flow through the AI 4-D cycle, as shown in Table 3.

Day	4-D Cycle Focus	Participants
Day 1: Discovery	Mobilize a systemic or systemwide inquiry into the positive core	• Engage in appreciative interviews • Reflect on interview highlights
Day 2: Dream	Envision the organization's greatest potential for positive influence and effect in the world.	• Share dreams collected during the interviews • Create and present dramatic enactments
Day 3: Design	Craft a set of propositions in which the positive core is boldly alive in all strategies, processes, systems, decisions, and collaborations.	• Draft provocative propositions (design statements) incorporating the positive core
Day 4: Destiny	Invite action inspired by the discovery, dream, and design days.	• Publicly declare intended actions and ask for support • Self-organized groups plan next steps

Table 3 AI 4–D Cycle and the AI Summit

Roadway Express: Moving from Good to Great

For seventy-five years, Roadway Express, headquartered in Akron, Ohio, has been a leading transporter of industrial, commercial, and retail goods and has offered a variety of innovative services to meet customer needs. In addition to seamless service between all fifty states, Canada, Mexico, and Puerto Rico, Roadway Express also offers export and import services to more than one hundred countries worldwide. With more than three hundred terminals throughout the U.S. and twenty-seven thousand people, Roadway is one of the largest LTL carriers in the nation and one of the region's most stable employers. In 2004, it combined with Yellow and is now the largest component of the new Yellow Roadway Corporation.

Four years ago, Roadway Express decided to launch a bold initiative to drive costs out and to more rapidly increase business by creating an organization with *leadership at every level*. Dock workers, truck drivers, stackers, and all levels of professionals would join with the senior management team at facilities across the network to conduct annual strategic planning, learn everything about the economics and financials of the business, and create new levels of partnership between the unions and the company as a whole. Roadway chose AI to ignite the change and to create a company in which everyone is engaged in the fundamentals of the business.

Roadway began holding AI Summits throughout its North American operations, realizing that to thrive in an industry in which net profit margins are less than 5 percent in a profitable year, each of its twenty-eight thousand employees must assume leadership responsibility. The results have been impressive. When the work began, Roadway stock was around $14 per share. In two years the stock rose to more than $40 per share, before any merger discussions with Yellow, whose stock was a much lower $24 per share. Following the merger in 2003, the combined company was valued at around $42 per share because of the strength of Roadway's improvements.

But beyond stock prices, many other measures have steadily improved at statistically significant levels, including operating ratios (the lowest in years) and well-documented overtime changes in survey data looking at measures of morale, levels of trust, clarity in focus and priority vision, commitment levels, and confidence in a new and better future. Many of the changes occurred during an economic downturn in the industry and have been traced to the power and effect of the new culture of engagement fostered by more than twenty large-scale Appreciative Inquiry AI Summits.

Jim Staley, Roadway's CEO, says he's seen tremendous employee involvement in task teams at terminals that have held AI Summits, and each team has produced results. "The Appreciative Inquiry approach unleashes tremendous power, tremendous enthusiasm, and gets people fully engaged in the right way in what we're trying to accomplish," Mr. Staley says. "It's not that we don't deal with the negative anymore," he explains. "But the value of AI is that, in anything we do, there's a positive foundation of strength to build on in addressing those problems."

A case in point was the AI Summit held at the Winston-Salem terminal. It was a whole-system strategic planning meeting, with more than three hundred truck drivers, dock workers, senior executives, teamsters, managers, and customers coming together across all boundaries to cocreate their business plan. A *Forbes* business writer, Joanne Gordon, surprised Roadway by asking if she could participate in the three-day event.

She was initially skeptical of the method and then clearly surprised. Her article described the business focus of the AI Summit along with the passion demonstrated by the dock workers and drivers:

> A team of short-haul drivers came up with twelve cost-cutting and revenue-generating ideas. One of the most ambitious: Have each of the thirty-two drivers in Winston-Salem deliver just one more customer order each hour. Using management data, the drivers calculated the that 288 additional daily shipments, at an average revenue of $212 each and with a 6 percent margin, would generate just about $1 million a year of operating costs.

At its analyst meeting several months later, on January 22, 2003, Roadway Corporation reported that revenues for the sixteen weeks constituting the company's fourth quarter were $1,074,110,000, up 25.7 percent when compared to revenues of $854,640,000 for the same period the previous year. For the fourth quarter of 2002, the company reported income from continuing operations of $25,923,000, or $1.37 per share (diluted), compared to income from continuing operations of $13,477,000, or $0.72 per share (diluted), for the fourth quarter of 2001. Operating ratios improved significantly and, according to later analysis, the employee-driven improvements translated into an additional $17 million in revenue for the year and $7 million annual profit.

The most telling finding is that the vast majority of improvements came from the facilities that had conducted at least one AI Summit. This is why, for example, when the merger of Yellow and Roadway took place, the AI Summit was chosen as a vehicle to bring the merger integration to a higher level. Synergy savings are estimated at $300 million, to be accelerated by the large group multistakeholder methods of AI. (It was through stories like this at Roadway that the U.S. Navy's Admiral Clark took notice and called on AI to create high-engagement planning methods for the Navy.)

The real story is about the sustainability of momentum, which can be traced to three things:

■ The AI Summit method has become a way of life. Roadway draws on the AI Summit design and approach for every major strategic change. In the past three years, Roadway has conducted more than sixty AI Summits.

■ The AI Summit method is effective because it engages all stakeholders in one collaborative planning process (creating thousands of ambassadors and saving time that hundreds of slower, small group meetings would require);

■ The capacity to do this type of high-engagement planning is now internalized in the company. More than ten thousand people have participated in at least one AI Summit.

The company's capacity has been widened throughout the system using an electronic and virtual architecture called the *core strength network*, with thousands of active members helping to speed the spread of every innovation and next practice throughout the system. In their last virtual meeting, more than three thousand people participated in sharing breakthroughs in the dock design in Akron; how drivers became salespersons and sold $5 million in new business in Winston-Salem, and how another terminal became the highest margin facility in the company. Although the core strength network is in its infancy, it is a great example of embedding AI as an everyday innovation accelerator. The next step is to support the network of strength sharing through a new software product called OvationNet, designed for ongoing online knowledge sharing and collaboration.

Chapter Six

Roles, Responsibilities, and Relationships

··

Successful change management requires the attention, focus, and commitment of large numbers of people. Our experience suggests that the more positive the focus of the change effort, the stronger the attraction to participate and the more likely people are to get involved and stay involved. Clarity of roles, responsibilities, and relationships creates channels of participation and supports active involvement of all stakeholders.

This chapter provides an overview of the roles, responsibilities, and relationships central to successful positive change. As you will see in Table 4, everyone has a role in creating positive change.

The Role of Leadership

The role of an organization's leadership is that of sponsors, or *positive change catalysts*. Leaders participate equally as one of the many essential voices at the table. Given the opportunity to listen to and hear the creative ideas, hopes, and dreams of their colleagues and organization stakeholders, leaders recognize that their job is to plant the seed and nurture the best in others. After the positive revolution begins, what it needs most is affirmation and a clear, open pathway for experimentation and innovation. Leadership must be present throughout the process, asking powerful, positive, value-based questions, expecting the best, and being truly curious about the hopes and dreams of organizational members. By modeling AI as a relational leadership practice, leaders send a clear and consistent message: positive change is the pathway to success around here.

Generally, a leadership advisory team is formed to provide guidance and resources to the process. The advisory team works closely with the AI consultant and the core team responsible for the ongoing planning, design, and delivery of the project. The leadership advisory team consists of three to six senior leaders committed to the success of the AI project.

The Role of an AI Consultant

As Table 4 shows, an AI consultant can support the process in four ways:

- Introduce AI to the organization and train people as internal agents of inquiry, interviewers, and AI facilitators.
- Design the overall project flow through the AI 4-D cycle, providing guidance about when and how to involve the optimum number of stakeholders.
- Facilitate AI activities throughout the process.
- Continually seek ways to give the process away, to support organizational members in making it their own.

To be successful, an AI consultant must view organizations as living spiritual-social systems—mysteries of creation to be nurtured and affirmed, not mechanistic or scientific operations with problems to be solved. They must be able to work in the energetically positive, continually seeking to discover what gives life to the organization and its members when they are at their best. And they must be skilled at seeing and bringing out the best of others.

	Before	During	After
Leadership	• Learn AI • Plant the AI seed	• Champion AI in the organization • Participate as an equal, essential voice	• Ask how might we take an AI approach to this? • Lead by affirmation
Consultants	• Introduce AI to the organization • Focus on the business case for AI	• Train groups in AI • Support the core team • Facilitate the AI process	• Assist the organization to integrate • AI into daily practices
Core team	• Learn AI	• Select affirmative topics • Create the interview guide • Determine the interview strategy • Communicate best stories	• Use AI as a daily practice
Participants	• Learn AI • Conduct interviews and be interviewed • Review interview stories and share best practices	• Engage in discovery and dialogue • Dare to dream • Design the ideal organization	• Integrate AI into existing processes and practices • Create new systems and structures using AI • Practice AI on a daily basis

Table 4 AI Roles and Responsibilities

The Role of the Core Team

The third role described in Table 4 is that of the core team. Stewardship of an organization-wide AI process generally rests with a core team selected for diverse backgrounds, functional experience, and organizational responsibility. The core team plans, designs, and oversees the entire process. It is responsible for creating the project's communication architecture, coordinating communication, and being sure that all members of the organization are well informed about the process and their opportunities to participate. The core team often selects and works with managers to identify people to be invited to conduct interviews, be interviewed, and attend various meetings. In essence, the core team guides the overall AI initiative and monitors its effect.

The Role of the Participants

The primary role of participants in an AI process is to be students of organizational life. AI engages all levels of an organization and its stakeholders in a cooperative learning and cocreation process. To be a student of organizational life emphasizes curiosity and learning in the most pragmatic sense. AI is the study of the best of what has been and what can be. In the process, best practices inspire action toward dreams for a collective future that are grounded in reality and hence believable and feasible.

AI is an invitation to a positive revolution, to meeting others who might otherwise be considered "them," and to learn and cocreate a world that works for all. AI participants are often surprised by how much they learn about themselves as well as others in the process. Openness to learning is often an exciting and life-giving outcome of AI.

Chapter Seven

Principles for a Positive Revolution

O ur undestanding of AI calls for a distinctive shift in human organizations and change. AI embodies both a philosophy and a methodology for change. In this chapter we present the five principles and scholarly streams of thought we consider central to AI. Familiarity with these principles will enable you to adapt Appreciative Inquiry to meet unique and challenging new situations and to create innovative practices of positive change.

The Constructionist Principle

The constructionist principle states the following:

Human knowledge and organizational destiny are interwoven. We are constantly involved in understanding and making sense of the people and world around us—doing strategic planning analysis, environmental scans, needs analysis, assessments and audits, surveys, focus groups, performance appraisals, and so on. To be effective executives, leaders, and change agents must be adept in the art of understanding, reading, and analyzing organizations as living, human constructions.

Constructionism[23] is an approach to human science that replaces the individual with the relationship as the locus of knowledge. Therefore, this approach is built around a keen appreciation of the power of language and discourse of all types (from words to metaphors to narrative forms and so on) to create our sense of reality—our sense of the true, the good, and the possible.

At stake are questions that pertain to the deepest dimensions of our being and humanity: how we know what we know, whose voices and interpretations matter, whether the world is governed by external laws independent of human choices and consciousness, and where is knowledge to be located. At stake are issues that are profoundly fundamental, not just for the future of social science but for the trajectory of all our lives.

Philosophically, constructionism involves a decisive shift in western intellectual tradition from *cogito ergo sum* to *communicamus ergo sum*. In practice, constructionism replaces absolutist claims or the final word with the never-ending collaborative quest to understand and construct options for better living. The purpose of inquiry, which is talked about as totally inseparable and intertwined with action, is the creation of generative theory, not so much mappings or explanations of yesterday's world but anticipatory articulations of tomorrow's possibilities. Constructionism, because of its emphasis on the communal basis of knowledge and its radical questioning of everything that is taken for granted as objective or seemingly immutable, invites us to find ways to increase the generative capacity of knowledge.

The Simultaneity Principle

The principle of simultaneity states the following:

> Inquiry and change are not separate moments, but are simultaneous. Inquiry is intervention. The seeds of change—the things people think and talk about, the things people discover and learn, and the things that inform dialogue and inspire images of the future—are implicit in the very first questions we ask. The questions we ask set the stage for what we find, and

what we discover (the data) becomes the linguistic material, the stories, out of which the future is conceived and constructed.

One of the most important things a change agent or practitioner does is to articulate questions. Instinctively, intuitively, and tacitly, we all know that research of any kind can, in a flash, profoundly alter the way we see ourselves, view reality, and conduct our lives. Consider the economic poll, or the questions that led to the discovery of the atom bomb, or the leaked surveys that create a riot at a unionized automobile plant in London. If we accept the proposition that patterns of social-organizational action are not fixed by nature in any direct biological or physical way and that human systems are made and imagined in relational settings by human beings (socially constructed), attention turns to the source of our ideas, our discourses, our researches—those are our questions. Alterations in linguistic practices, including the linguistic practice of crafting questions, hold profound implications for changes in social practice.

When we consider that inquiry and change are a simultaneous moment, we begin reflecting anew. It is not so much, "Is my question leading to right or wrong answers?" but rather, "What effect is my question having on our lives together. Is it helping to generate conversations about the good, the better, the possible. Is it strengthening our relationships?"

The Poetic Principle

The poetic principle states:

> A metaphor here is that human organizations are a lot more like an open book than, say, a machine. An organization's story is constantly being coauthored. Pasts, presents, and futures are endless sources of learning, inspiration, and interpretation, like the endless interpretive possibilities in a poem or a literary text. The implication is that we can study virtually any topic related to human experience. We can inquire into the nature of alienation or joy, enthusiasm or low morale, efficiency or excess, in any human organization.

Constuctionism reminds us that the world out there does not dictate our topics of inquiry. Rather, the topics are themselves social artifacts, products of social processes (cultural habits, professional ways, power relations). AI says let us make sure we are not just reproducing the same worlds over and over again because of the simple and boring repetition of our questions (not one more morale survey). AI also says, with excitement, that there are great gains to be made in linking the means and ends of inquiry. Options now begin to multiply. For example, in talks with great leaders of nongovernmental organizations (such as Save the Children and World Vision), we have begun to appreciate the profound joy that CEOs feel as servant leaders and the role this *positive effect* plays in creating healthy organizations. Does this mean that executive joy has something to do with good leadership or healthy human systems? Why aren't we including this topic in our change efforts? What might happen if we did?

The Anticipatory Principle

The anticipatory principle states the following:

> Our positive images of the future lead our positive actions. This is the increasingly energizing basis and presupposition of Appreciative Inquiry. The infinite human resource we have for generating constructive organizational change is our collective imagination and discourse about the future.

The image of the future guides the current behavior of any organization. Much like a movie projector on a screen, human systems are forever projecting a horizon of expectations ahead of themselves. Their talk in the hallways, the metaphors and language they use, bring the future powerfully into the present as a mobilizing agent. Inquiring in ways that redefine anticipatory reality[24]—creating positive images together—may be the most important aspect of any change process.

In studies about the effects of positive imagery from placebo studies in medicine, to studies of the Pygmalion dynamic in the classroom, to studies of the rise and fall of cultures, to research into the relationships between optimism and health, to studies of ways for accelerating learning, to analysis of the importance of positive inner dialogue to personal and relational well-being, to research on positive mood states and effective decision making, and to theories on how noticing even small wins can reverberate throughout a system and change the world—the conclusions are converging on something Aristotle said. "A vivid imagination compels the whole body to obey it."

The Positive Principle

The positive principle states:

> Building and sustaining momentum for change requires large amounts of positive affect and social bonding—things like hope, excitement, inspiration, caring, camaraderie, sense of urgent purpose, and sheer joy in creating something meaningful together. We find that the more positive the question we ask, the more long-lasting and successful the change effort. The major thing a change agent can do that makes a difference is to craft and ask unconditionally positive questions.

Our experience shows that we need no longer be hesitant about bringing affirmative language more carefully and prominently into business. It is a much healthier and more effective way of approaching change management. A theory of the affirmative basis of human action and organizing is emerging from many quarters, including social constructionism, image theory, conscious evolution, athletics, and healthcare. And taken together, we believe, it is making traditional change management traditions look obsolete.

In the past five years, the practice of AI has led to the articulation of additional principles. In *The Power of Appreciative Inquiry*, consultants Diana Whitney and Amanda Trosten-Bloom add three principles they believe are essential to successful large-scale positive change: wholeness, enactment, and free choice. Professors Frank Barrett and Ron Fry, in *Appreciative Inquiry: A Positive Approach to Building Cooperative Capacity*, add the narrative principle as central to Appreciative Inquiry and other social constructionist processes of change management.

Chapter Eight

Conditions for Success: The Liberation of Power

For nearly two decades, we have watched as organizations and communities around the globe have experienced extraordinary transformations using Appreciative Inquiry for organization and social change. Several years ago, having tracked this consistent success in Nutrimental Foods, GTE, Hunter Douglas WFD, and others, Appreciative Inquiry consultants and authors Diana Whitney and Amanda Trosten-Bloom began wondering what created the conditions for AI's success. More specifically, they began asking, Why do people get so excited and want to participate in Appreciative Inquiry? Why does participation so readily lead to positive results, such as innovation, productivity, employee satisfaction, and profitability? What creates the space for people to be their best at work and for personal transformation? And what are the conditions that foster cooperation throughout a whole system of highly diverse groups of people?

In keeping with the spirit of Appreciative Inquiry, they sought answers to these questions by conducting an inquiry into *why Appreciative Inquiry works*. They created a set of questions, held focus groups, and conducted formal and informal interviews in several organizations, most notably Hunter Douglas Window Fashions Division.

Their key finding is that Appreciative Inquiry works by generating six essential conditions in an organization that together liberate or unleash personal and organizational power (potential). Having experienced this liberation and the effect it has on their lives and the world around them, people are permanently transformed.

Whitney and Trosten-Bloom named the conditions through which AI liberates power and unleashes human potential the *six freedoms*. Following is a description of each, along with quotes from employees of Hunter Douglas Window Fashions Division and others. These are the voices of the organizationally liberated, describing the conditions that bring out their best.[25]

Freedom to Be Known in Relationship

AI creates a context in which people are free to be known in relationship. Human identity forms and evolves in relationships. Yet all too often in work settings, people are related to as their role rather than as a human being. Appreciative Inquiry interrupts the cycle of depersonalization that masks people's sense of being and belonging. It offers people the chance to truly know one another, both as unique individuals and as a part of the web of relationships.

Appreciative Inquiry doesn't only build relationships. It also levels the playing field and builds bridges across boundaries of power and authority. One machinist exclaimed, "Appreciative Inquiry blew the communication gap wide open." Similarly, John Cade, a printer, commented on the ways in which Appreciative Inquiry in general—and the interviews in particular—help to make other people and their ideas more accessible: "Appreciative Inquiry gave us opportunities to be known across the boundaries. As our inquiry got fully under way, other people became excited, just like me. I didn't feel alone. For the first time, it was me with the world."

Freedom to Be Heard

AI makes a space in which people are free to be heard. A person can listen without truly hearing or getting to know the other. Being heard, on the other hand, requires someone to listen with sincere curiosity, empathy, and compassion. It requires an openness to know and understand another person's story.

Through one-on-one appreciative interviews, people who might otherwise feel ignored and without voice are invited to come forward with information, ideas, and innovations that are subsequently put into action throughout the organization. In the process, people feel heard, recognized, and valued.

Mark Maier, the supervisor of a technical maintenance group, initiated an inquiry among his team's internal customers (engineers, technical support staff, and others). He and his staff conducted interviews and collected stories of exceptional service. They invited people to dream about the service that they'd always wanted and to describe it in detail. In the process, they built relationships across functions, in particular between engineering and technical support. Being heard brought the group to life.

Freedom to Dream in Community

AI opens the opportunity for people to be free to dream in community. In today's complex world, visionary leadership means unleashing the dreams of people at all levels of the organization. It means creating organizations as safe places where large, diverse groups of people dream and share their dreams, in dialogue with one another.

In American Baptist International Ministries, for example, several months of interviews with more than twelve hundred stakeholders worldwide yielded a vision of an entirely new model of service: from *sending people out* to do good, to *linking people and organizations of similar intent* around the globe. This vision was so compelling—and its momentum so great—that by the first anniversary of the summit, close to thirty new initiatives were launched using this "sister organization" model as a template. Then, in the two years that followed, close to two hundred new initiatives, or dreams, unfolded. Consultant Jim Ludema described the community's dreaming as "an unleashing of energy and power that was already there. It was a positive explosion waiting to happen."

Freedom to Choose to Contribute

AI establishes an environment where people are free to choose to contribute. Work can separate us from what matters most to us; or it can provide a forum for enacting and realizing our deepest calling. Freedom of choice liberates power, but it also leads to commitment and a hunger for learning. When people choose to do a project and commit to others to do it, they get creative and determined. They will do whatever it takes and learn whatever is needed to do the job. For example, a front-line employee who had volunteered to lead an innovation team went to her personnel department and asked for coaching. She declared that she needed to learn to facilitate meetings and help her team make decisions for them to succeed. Her determination paid off for the team, the organization, and herself. The team's project was finished in record time and led to significant process improvements in the company. She was promoted to a supervisory position and her new team is thriving with her leadership.

Freedom to Act with Support

AI provides the context for people to be free to act with support. To act with support is the quintessential act of positive interdependence. When people know that large numbers of people care about their work and are anxious to cooperate, they feel safe to experiment, innovate, and learn. In other words, whole-system support stimulates people to take on challenges and draws people into acts of cooperation that bring forth their best.

To break through years of apathy and distrust, John Deere Harvester Works initiated a five-day summit, the last two days of which were focused on what they called tactical implementation. Participants selected ten projects that they believed were critically important. Then, to their surprise, they began working with one another right there in the summit to plan, line up resources, and initiate the projects.

When people are truly free to act with support, their contributions are profound and their lessons sometimes surprising. Tina LaGrange at Hunter Douglas shows us that this freedom liberates individual and organizational power—even when the intended actions fail to reach fruition. "My coworkers and I worked hard to make the case for and create a cross-training program. It was ready for implementation, and then . . . nobody signed up! I was deeply disappointed but ultimately okay. In the end, the only thing I really accomplished was getting an answer: People simply weren't that interested. But an answer was a big thing. It meant that I had the power to get an answer."

Freedom to Be Positive

AI opens the way for people to be free to be positive. In organizations today, it is simply not the norm to have fun, be happy, or be positive. Despite the pain it causes, people allow themselves to be swept away in collective currents of negativity. A long-term employee of an organization mired in deficit discourse shared the following with dismay: "I have ulcers because of this negative thinking and talking. Every day I come to work and hear nothing but complaints and criticism and blaming. I hate coming to work."

Over and over again, people tell us that Appreciative Inquiry works, in part, because it gives people permission to feel positive and be proud of their working experiences. The effect of Appreciative Inquiry is so strong and powerful that it can even transform deficit discourse and negative thinking. In the words of one employee, "I am a very positive thinker, so this suits me very well. But I believe this process is powerful enough to influence all of the staff, not just those of us who are already this way."

The Liberation of Power Leads to Positive Change

Appreciative Inquiry works because it unleashes all of the six freedoms over the course of just one complete 4-D cycle. It creates a surge of power and energy that, once liberated, won't be recontained. A supervisor at Hunter Douglas said, "As people tried and got results, they gained confidence. That led to five times as much input, and the desire to get more involved." In short, according to Whitney and Trosten-Bloom, through the liberation of power, Appreciative Inquiry creates a self-perpetuating momentum for positive change—a positive revolution.

Conclusion

A ppreciative Inquiry (AI) is the beginning of an adventure. The urge and call to the positive revolution has been sounded by many people and many organizations, and it will take many more to fully explore the vast vistas that are now appearing on the horizon.

We are infants in understanding appreciative processes of knowing and social construction. Yet we see with increasingly clarity that the world is ready to leap beyond methodologies of deficit-based change and enter a domain that is lifecentric. AI theory states that organizations are centers of human relatedness, first and foremost, and relationships thrive where there is an appreciative eye—when people see the best in one another, share their dreams and ultimate concerns in affirming ways, and are connected in full voice to create not just new worlds but better worlds. The velocity and largely informal spread of appreciative learning suggests a growing disenchantment with exhausted theories of change, especially those wedded to vocabularies of human deficit, and a corresponding urge to work with people, groups, and organizations in more constructive, positive, life-affirming, and even spiritual ways. AI is more than a simple 4-D cycle of discovery, dream, design, and destiny; what is being introduced is something deeper at the core.

Perhaps our inquiry must become the positive revolution we want to see in the world. Albert Einstein's words clearly compel: "There are only two ways to live your life. One is as though nothing is a miracle. The other is as though everything is a miracle."

Notes

....

[1] Camerson, K.S., Dutton, J.E., and Quinn, R.E. (Editors), *Positive Organizational Scholarship*. San Francisco, CA: Berrett-Koehler, 2003.

[2] In the eighteen years since the theory and vision for *Appreciative Inquiry Into Organizational Life* was published (Cooperrider and Srivastva, 1987), literally thousands of people have been involved in cocreating new practices for doing AI and for bringing the spirit and methodology of AI into organizations all over the world.

[3] In 1999, GTE and Bell Atlantic merged, resulting in the formation of Verizon. We worked initially and extensively with GTE and continued with Verizon after the merger.

[4] GTE received the ASTD award in 1997 and went on to apply and gain benefit from Appreciative Inquiry in a wide range of settings, such as enhancing call center effectiveness, launching an innovative union-management partnership, and building an appreciative front-line leadership program. After the merger with Bell Atlantic and the creation of Verizon, Appreciative Inquiry was introduced to the companywide diversity network in support of a strength-based approach to diversity.

[5] Fry, R., Barrett, F., Seiling, J., and Whitney, D. (Editors). *Appreciative Inquiry and Organizational Transformation: Reports from the Field*. Westport, CN: Quorum Books, 2002.

[6] White, T.W. "Working in Interesting Times." In *Vital Speeches of the Day*, vol. LXII, no. 15 (1996), pp. 472-474.

[7] White, 1996.

[8] Hubbard, B.M. Conscious Evolution: Awaking the Power or our Social Potential. Novato, Calif. New Word Library, 1998.

[9] Bushe, G.R. *Clear Leadership*. Palo Alto, CA: Davies-Black Publishing, 2001.

[10] Chin, A. (1998) Future Visions. Journal of Organization and Change Management. (Spring); Curran M. (1991). Appreciative Inquiry: A Third Wave Approach to O.D. Vision/Action, December, 12-14.

[11] Gergen, K.J. *Realities and Relationships*. Cambridge, MA: Harvard University Press, 1994.

[12] Barrett, E.J., Creating appreciative learning cultures. *Organizational Dynamics*, 24(1), 36-49.

[13] Deal, T.E. and Kennedy, A.A. *Corporate Cultures: The Rites and Rituals of Corporate Life*. Reading, MA: Addison-Wesley Publishing Company, 1982.

[14] Ludema, J.D., Whitney, D., Mohr, B.J., and Griffin, T.J. *The Appreciative Inquiry Summit: A Practitioner's Guide for Leading Large-Group Change*. San Francisco, CA: Berrett-Koehler Publishers, Inc., 2003.

[15] Anderson, H., Gergen, K.J., McNamee, S., Cooperrider, D., Gergen, M., and Whitney, D. *The Appreciative Organization*. Taos, NM: Taos Institute Publishing, 2001.

[16] Hock, D. *Birth of the Chaordic Age*. San Francisco, CA: Berrett-Koehler Publishers, Inc., 1999.

[17] For more on the United Religions Initiative, go to www.uri.org.

[18] Gibbs, C. and Mahe, Sally *Birth of a Global Community: Appreciative Inquiry in Action*. Bedford Heights, OH: Lakeshore Communications, Inc., 2004.

[19] Chapter 2 of *The Power of Appreciative Inquiry*, written by Diana Whitney and Amanda Trosten-Bloom, provides an excellent overview of the forms of engagement for applying Appreciative Inquiry.

[20] Whitney, D. and Trosten-Bloom, A. *The Power of Appreciative Inquiry*. San Francisco, CA: Berrett-Koehler Publishers, Inc., 2003.

[21] Ludema, J.D., Whitney, D., Mohr, B.J. and Griffin, T.J. *The Appreciative Inquiry Summit: A Practitioner's Guide for Leading Large-Group Change*. San Francisco, CA: Berrett-Koehler Publishers, Inc., 2003.

22 Ludema, J.D., Whitney, D., Mohr, B.J. and Griffin, T.J. *The Appreciative Inquiry Summit: A Practitioner's Guide for Leading Large-Group Change*. San Francisco, CA: Berrett-Koehler Publishers, Inc., 2003.

23 In our view, the finest work in this area, indeed a huge extension of the most radical ideas in Lewinian thought, can be found in Ken Gergen's *Toward Transformation in Social Knowledge* (1982) and *Realities and Relationships: Soundings in Social Construction* (1994). What Gergen does in both of these is to synthesize the essential whole of the post-modern ferment, crucially take it beyond disenchantment with the old, and offer alternative conceptions of knowledge, fresh discourses on human functioning, new vistas for human science, and exciting directions for approaching change.

24 Cooperrider, D.L. "Positive Image Positive Action: The Affirmative Basis of Organizing." *In Appreciative Management and Leadership*, Rev. S. Srivastva and D.L. Cooperrider, (editors) pp.91-125. Cleveland, Ohio: Williams Publishing Co., 1999.

25 Whitney, D. and Trosten-Bloom, A. *The Power of Appreciative Inquiry*. San Francisco, CA: Berrett-Koehler Publishers, Inc., 2003.

Questions for Applying AI

To gain additional value from this book, consider discussing it with others. Here are some questions you might find useful as you explore Appreciative Inquiry and its application to your organization or community.

1. What attracted you to read about Appreciative Inquiry? What fascinated you? What ideas do you have for how AI might be used to help your organization or community achieve its mission and goals?

2. Think about your organization or community with an appreciative eye. What are the positive factors that give it life when it is at its best? That give life to your customer relations? That give life to your capacity for cooperation and partnership? That give life to your leadership?

3. What do you want more of in your organization or community? What dreams do you have for its greater health and vitality? How might Appreciative Inquiry be applied to help you realize these dreams?

4. Appreciative Inquiry works its way into an organization
or a community's communication system. It creates a
narrative-rich culture through stories, best practices,
and other forms of knowledge. In what areas is greater
sharing of information essential to success in your
organization or community? What benefits might result
from broader awareness of stories of best practices?

5. What applications of AI are most relevant to your
organization or community: Customer service,
profits, diversity, technology integration, new product
development, or union management relations? What
topics would you select to guide the inquiry? Who
would you involve?

6. An AI summit is generally four days long and involves
all stakeholders. How would this approach work to
address a strategic issue in your organization? What
would be the most desirable outcome of an AI summit
on this issue? How would the creative involvement of all
stakeholders benefit the organization?

Are you ready for the positive revolution?

Where to Go for More Information

B ecause our focus has been to give you an introduction to Appreciative Inquiry, we want you to know where to go for more information. Following are web sites, books, and articles that can help you develop a more in-depth understanding of AI.

Web Sites

Case Western Reserve University

Weatherhead School of Management

www.cwru.edu

216-368-2215

Graduate studies, research, and executive education

Corporation for Positive Change

www.positivechange.org

505-751-1232

Change management consultation, AI certificate program, appreciative leadership development, and keynote speeches

Taos Institute

www.taosinstitute.net

888-999-TAOS

Conferences, graduate studies, and workshops

AI Commons

http://ai.cwru.edu

Articles, sample materials, and case studies about AI

AI Practitioner

www.aipractitioner.com

International AI newsletter

Books on Appreciative Inquiry by the Authors

Appreciative Leadership and Management, Editors: S. Srivastva, D. Cooperrider, and Associates, Jossey-Bass, 1990

Appreciative Inquiry: Collaborating for Change (booklet), D. Cooperrider and D. Whitney, Berrett-Koehler, 1999

Appreciative Inquiry Handbook, D. Cooperrider, D. Whitney, and J. Stavros, Lakeshore Communications and Berrett Koehler Communications, 2003

The Power of Appreciative Inquiry, D. Whitney and A. Trosten-Bloom, Berrett-Koehler Communications, 2002

The Appreciative Inquiry Summit, J. Ludema, D. Whitney, B. Mohr, and T. Griffin, Berrett-Koehler Communications, 2003

Advances in Appreciative Inquiry, Editors: D. Cooperrider and M. Avital, Elsevier Science, 2004

The Encyclopedia of Positive Questions, D. Whitney, A. Trosten-Bloom, B. Kaplin, and D. Cooperrider, Lakeshore Communications, 2002

Appreciative Team Building, D. Whitney, A. Trosten-Bloom, J. Cherney, and R. Fry, iUniverse, 2005

Positive Approaches to Peacebuilding, Editors: C. Sampson, M. Abu-Nimer, C. Liebler, and D. Whitney, PACT Publications, 2004

Appreciative Inquiry and Organizational Transformation: Reports from the Field, Editors: R. Fry, F. Barrett, J. Seiling, and D. Whitney, Quorum Books, 2002

The Appreciative Organization, H. Anderson, D. Cooperrider, K. Gergen, M. Gergen, S. McNamee, and D. Whitney, Taos Institute Publishing, 2000

Appreciative Inquiry: Rethinking Human Organization Toward a Positive Theory of Change, D. Cooperrider, P. Sorenson, D. Whitney, and T. Yaeger, Stipes Publishing, 2000

Appreciative Inquiry: An Emerging Direction for Organization Development, Editors: D. Cooperrider, P. Sorenson, T. Yaeger, and D. Whitney, Stipes Publishing, 2005

Index

The Authors

....

David L. Cooperrider

David L. Cooperrider is Professor and Chairman of the Department of Organizational Behavior at the Weatherhead School of Management, Case Western Reserve University. He is past President of the National Academy of Management's OD Division and has lectured and taught at Stanford, University of Chicago, Katholieke University in Belgium, MIT, University of Michigan, Cambridge, and others.

David serves as researcher and advisor to a wide variety of organizations, including Yellow Roadway Corp., Green Mountain Coffee Roasters, McCann-Erickson, Nutrimental Foods, World Vision, Cleveland Clinic, American Red Cross, and United Way of America. Most of the projects are inspired by Appreciative Inquiry. His founding work in this area is creating a positive revolution in the leadership of change; it is helping companies all over the world discover the power of the strength-based approaches to planning and multistakeholder cooperation. For example, Admiral Clark, the CNO of the Navy, recently met with David to bring AI into the Navy for a multiyear project on "Bold and Enlightened Naval Leadership." And in June 2004, Cooperrider was asked by the United Nations Global Compact to design and facilitate a historic, unprecedented summit meeting between Kofi Annan and five hundred business leaders to "unite the strengths of markets with the authority of universal ideals to make globalization work for everyone."

David often serves as meeting speaker and leader of large-group, interactive conference events. His dynamic ideas have been published in *Administrative Science Quarterly*, *Human Relations*, *Journal of Applied Behavioral Science*, and *The OD Practitioner* and in research series such as *Advances in Strategic Management*. More popularly, his work has been covered by *The New York Times*, *Forbes Magazine*, *Science*, *Fast Company*, *Fortune*, *Christian Science Monitor*, *San Francisco Chronicle*, and others. He has been recipient of *Best Paper of the Year Awards* at the Academy of Management and top researcher of the year at Case, and numerous clients have received awards for their work with Appreciative Inquiry. Among his highest honors, David was invited to design a series of dialogues among twenty-five of the world's top religious leaders, started by His Holiness the Dalai Lama, who said, "If only the world's religious leaders could just know each other, the world will be a better place." Using AI, the group has had meetings in Jerusalem and at the Carter Center with President Jimmy Carter. David was recognized in 2000 as among the "top ten visionaries" in the field by *Training Magazine* and in 2004 received the highest award from the American Society for Training and Development, the "Distinguished Contribution to Workplace Learning and Performance Award."

David has published nine books, including *Appreciative Inquiry* (with Diana Whitney) and *Organizational Courage and Executive Wisdom* and *Appreciative Leadership and Management* (both with Suresh Srivastva). David is editor of a new academic book series titled *Advances in Appreciative Inquiry* (with Michel Avital) published by Elsevier Science. David can be reached at David.Cooperrider@Case.edu.

Diana Whitney

Dr. Diana Whitney is President of the Corporation for Positive Change and a Distinguished Consulting Faculty at Saybrook Graduate School and Research Center. She is a social innovator and pioneer in the emerging field of positive organization change. She is a highly recognized international consultant, a sought-after leadership advisor, and a frequently called upon keynote speaker on subjects related to Appreciative Inquiry and large-scale organization and community transformation, appreciative leadership development, and spiritual cultivation. Diana is a fellow of the World Business Academy, a founder and director of the Taos Institute, and a founding advisor to the United Religions Initiative.

Diana teaches, speaks, and consults throughout the Americas, Europe, and Asia. She has lectured and taught at Antioch University, Case Western Reserve University, and Benedictine University in the U.S., Kensington Consultation Center and Ashridge Management Institute in London, Eisher Institute in India, Croma Business Academy in Croatia, and others.

She has authored and edited twelve books and numerous articles on Appreciative Inquiry, including the highly acclaimed guide to positive change: *The Power of Appreciative Inquiry* with Amanda Trosten-Bloom and the *Appreciative Inquiry Handbook* with David Cooperrider and Jackie Stavros. In 2004 Diana received the Organization Development Network's Larry Porter Award for excellence in writing.

Dr. Whitney's consulting focuses on the use of Appreciative Inquiry for corporate culture change, strategic planning, large-scale organization transformation, merger integration, partnership building, leadership development, and service excellence. Her clients span the globe, and include British Airways, Hunter Douglas WFD, Merck LA, CapGemini, Verizon (GTE), First Caribbean International Bank, Ameriquest, Johnson & Johnson, Sandia National Laboratory, and Nevada Child Welfare Services. Her work with GTE received the American Society for Training and Development's Outstanding Organization Change Award. Recognized as a leading practitioner of positive change and an inspirational thought leader, Diana has been called upon by international professional associations as a keynote speaker to introduce positive change practices to the fields of public participation, mediation, systemic management, executive education, public relations, and interfaith leadership.

Dr. Whitney received her Ph.D. from Temple University in the field of Organizational Communication. Her early research into the dissemination of educational innovations funded by the National Institute of Education created an agenda for the ongoing development of educational R&D laboratories throughout the United States.

Diana continues to serve as an advisor to the United Religions Initiative, a global interfaith organization dedicated to peace and cooperation among people of diverse religions, faiths, and spiritual traditions. She lives in Taos, New Mexico and can be reached at diana@positivechange.org.

.

Berrett–Koehler
Publishers

Berrett-Koehler is an independent publisher dedicated to an ambitious mission: *Connecting people and ideas to create a world that works for all.*

We believe that the solutions to the world's problems will come from all of us, working at all levels: in our organizations, in our society, and in our own lives. Our BK Business books help people make their organizations more humane, democratic, diverse, and effective (we don't think there's any contradiction there). Our BK Currents books offer pathways to creating a more just, equitable, and sustainable society. Our BK Life books help people create positive change in their lives and align their personal practices with their aspirations for a better world.

All of our books are designed to bring people seeking positive change together around the ideas that empower them to see and shape the world in a new way.

And we strive to practice what we preach. At the core of our approach is Stewardship, a deep sense of responsibility to administer the company for the benefit of all of our stakeholder groups including authors, customers, employees, investors, service providers, and the communities and environment around us. Everything we do is built around this and our other key values of quality, partnership, inclusion, and sustainability.

This is why we are both a B-Corporation and a California Benefit Corporation—a certification and a for-profit legal status that require us to adhere to the highest standards for corporate, social, and environmental performance.

We are grateful to our readers, authors, and other friends of the company who consider themselves to be part of the BK Community. We hope that you, too, will join us in our mission.

A BK Business Book

We hope you enjoy this BK Business book. BK Business books pioneer new leadership and management practices and socially responsible approaches to business. They are designed to provide you with groundbreaking and practical tools to transform your work and organizations while upholding the triple bottom line of people, planet, and profits. High-five!

To find out more, visit **www.bkconnection.com**.

Berrett–Koehler
BK Publishers

Connecting people and ideas
to create a world that works for all

Dear Reader,

Thank you for picking up this book and joining our worldwide community of Berrett-Koehler readers. We share ideas that bring positive change into people's lives, organizations, and society.

To welcome you, we'd like to offer you a free e-book. You can pick from among twelve of our bestselling books by entering the promotional code **BKP92E** here: http://www.bkconnection.com/welcome.

When you claim your free e-book, we'll also send you a copy of our e-newsletter, the *BK Communiqué*. Although you're free to unsubscribe, there are many benefits to sticking around. In every issue of our newsletter you'll find

- A free e-book
- Tips from famous authors
- Discounts on spotlight titles
- Hilarious insider publishing news
- A chance to win a prize for answering a riddle

Best of all, our readers tell us, "Your newsletter is the only one I actually read." So claim your gift today, and please stay in touch!

Sincerely,

Charlotte Ashlock
Steward of the BK Website

Questions? Comments? Contact me at bkcommunity@bkpub.com.